DATE DUE		
MAY 2 5 AUG		
AUG 1 5 2005		

Valentine's Day

by Mari C. Schuh

Consulting Editor: Gail Saunders-Smith, Ph.D.

Consultant: Alexa Sandmann, Ed.D.
Professor of Literacy
The University of Toledo
Member, National Council for the Social Studies

Pebble Books

an imprint of Capstone Press
Mankato, Minnesota

Pebble Books are published by Capstone Press
151 Good Counsel Drive, P.O. Box 669, Mankato, Minnesota 56002
http://www.capstone-press.com

1 2 3 4 5 6 07 06 05 04 03 02

Library of Congress Cataloging-in-Publication Data
Schuh, Mari C., 1975–
    Valentine's Day / by Mari C. Schuh.
    p. cm.—(Holidays and celebrations)
    Includes bibliographical references and index.
    ISBN 0-7368-0982-1
    1. Valentine's Day—Juvenile literature. [1. Valentine's Day. 2. Holidays.] I. Title.
II. Series.
GT4925 .S38 2002
394.2618—dc21   00-013247

Summary: Simple text and photographs describe the history of Valentine's Day and
how it is celebrated.

Note to Parents and Teachers

The Holidays and Celebrations series supports national social
studies standards related to culture. This book describes Valentine's
Day and illustrates how it is celebrated. The photographs support
early readers in understanding the text. The repetition of words and
phrases helps early readers learn new words. This book also
introduces early readers to subject-specific vocabulary words, which
are defined in the Words to Know section. Early readers may need
assistance to read some words and to use the Table of Contents,
Words to Know, Read More, Internet Sites, and Index/Word List
sections of the book.

Table of Contents

Valentine's Day is on February 14. This holiday honors love and friendship.

No one is sure how
Valentine's Day started.
Some people believe
the holiday honors
a priest named Valentine.

8

Some Valentine's
Day traditions may
come from the ancient
Romans. They held
a festival every February.
They celebrated the
coming of spring.

Red, white, and pink are Valentine's Day colors. The heart shape is a Valentine's Day symbol.

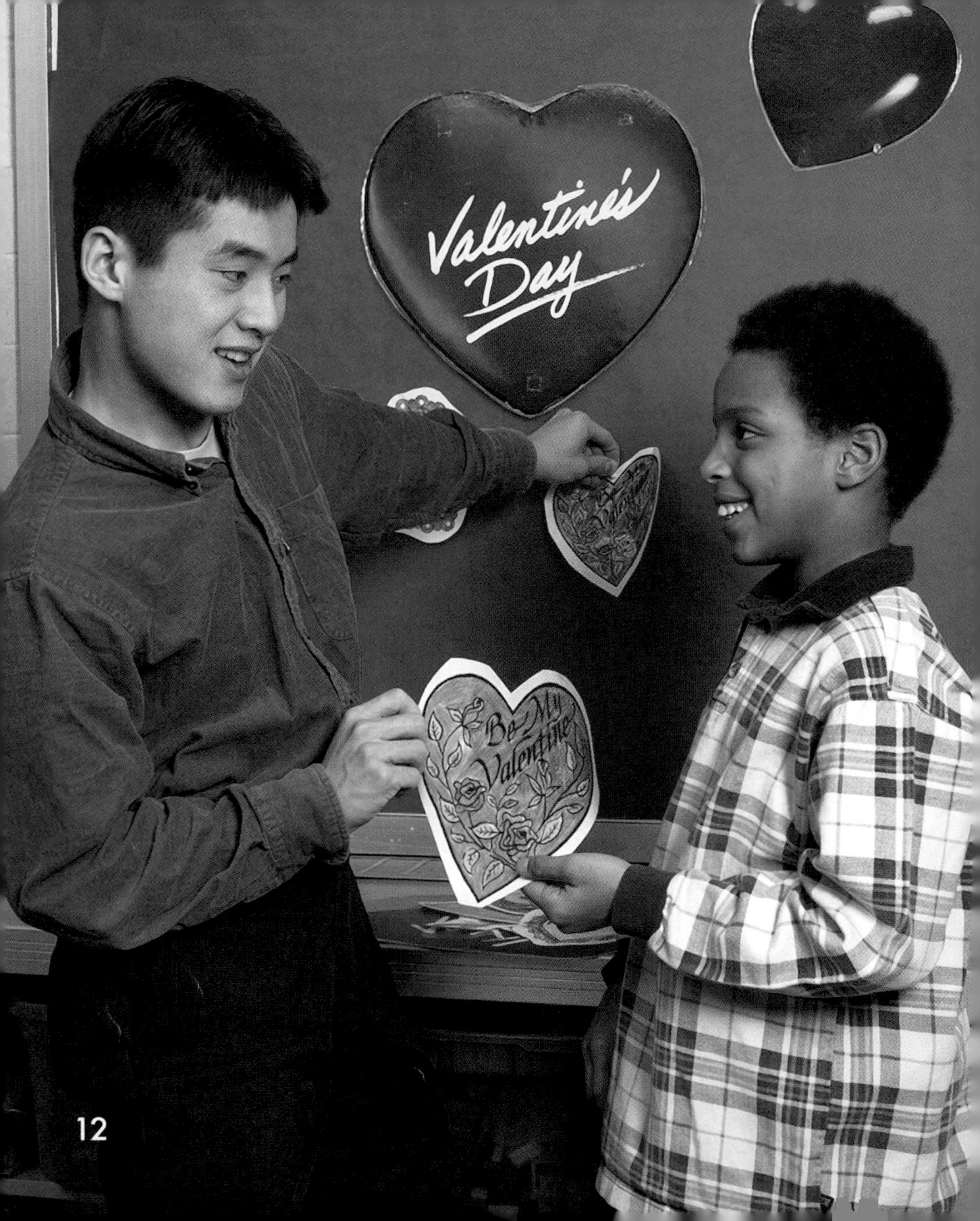
Valentine's Day
Be My Valentine

Some students and teachers decorate their classrooms for Valentine's Day.

Some friends send
valentines to each other.

Some families make
Valentine's Day cookies.

Some people give candy and flowers to people they love.

People celebrate love
and friendship
on Valentine's Day.

ancient—from a time long ago; some Valentine's Day traditions may have come from ancient Romans.

decorate—to add things to a room or an object to make it look nice

festival—a celebration or a holiday; some Valentine's Day traditions may have come from a Roman festival called Lupercalia.

priest—a member of a church who leads church services and performs religious rites

Roman—a person who lives in Rome; Rome is a city in Italy.

symbol—an object that stands for something else; the heart shape is a symbol of Valentine's Day.

tradition—a custom, idea, or belief that is passed from one generation to the next

valentine—a card given to someone on Valentine's Day

Read More

Klingel, Cynthia and Robert B. Noyed. *Valentine's Day.* Wonder Books. Chanhassen, Minn.: Child's World, 2001.

Marx, David F. *Valentine's Day.* Rookie Read-about Holidays. New York: Children's Press, 2001.

Rau, Dana Meachen. *Valentine's Day.* A True Book. New York: Children's Press, 2001.

Internet Sites

The Story of Valentine's Day
http://www.holidays.net/amore/story.html

Valentine's Day Resources for Kids and Teachers
http://www.kiddyhouse.com/Valentines/Valentines.html

Valentine's Fun at Kids Domain
http://www.kidsdomain.com/holiday/val

Index/Word List

Word Count: 109
Early-Intervention Level: 14

Credits
Heather Kindseth, cover designer; Kia Bielke, production designer; Kimberly Danger, photo researcher

Capstone Press/Gary Sundermeyer, cover, 1, 4, 10, 12, 14, 16, 18
Michael Krasowitz/FPG International LLC, 20
North Wind Picture Archives, 6, 8

Special thanks to Jane Schuette of Le Sueur, Minnesota, for providing props for photos in this book.